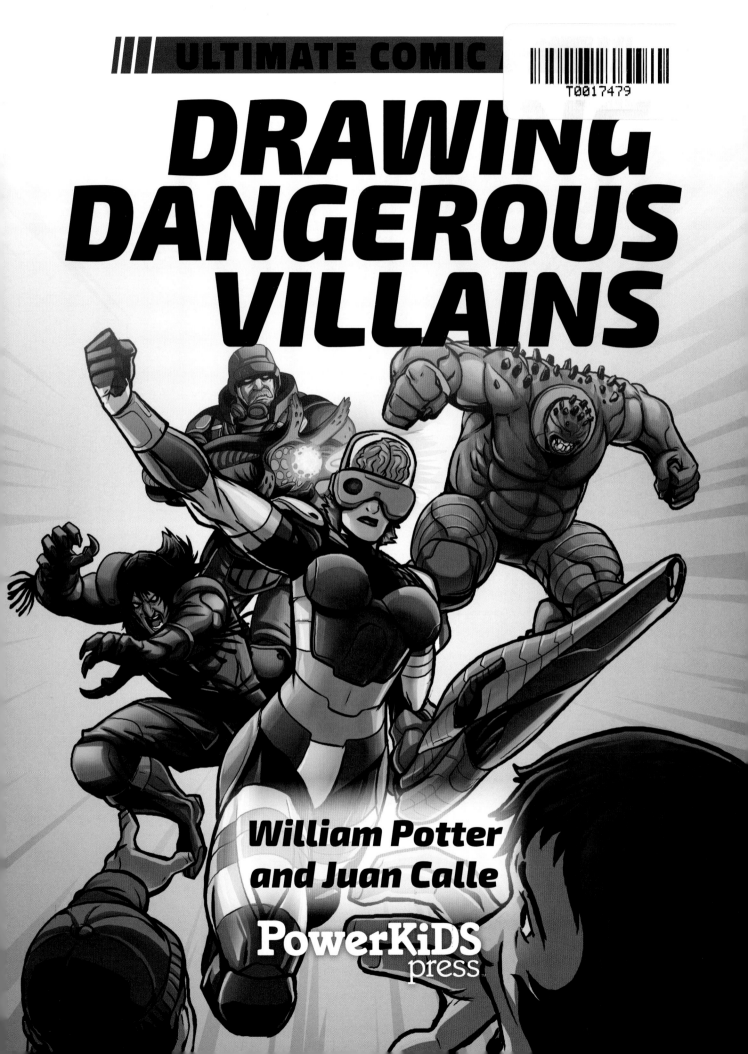

ULTIMATE COMIC ART

T0017479

DRAWING DANGEROUS VILLAINS

**William Potter
and Juan Calle**

PowerKiDS
press

CONTENTS

CITY IN TROUBLE

Every comic needs a great villain for the hero to battle against! We'll show you how to create your own nightmare characters and a comic strip to tell their strange stories.

COMIC CHARACTERS

This book is packed with ideas and guides to help you make up your own characters for incredible adventures. We'll show you the basics for bringing your characters to life and how to put them into a comic strip for all to see.

FIRST STEPS

We're going to focus on villains—daring wrongdoers, intent on causing trouble in the peaceful city. Coming up, there are guides on drawing anatomy and on materials to use. There's also advice on creating characters and scenes of chaos, and on using facial expressions to make wild creatures seem lifelike.

Four venomous villains have joined forces, bringing mayhem to Capital City! Take them on by designing your own wild weapons, power blasts, and explosions.

GETTING STARTED

PENCILS

Drawing pencils come in various hardnesses. H pencils are harder and B pencils are softer. A 2H pencil is good for making light marks that don't smudge, while a 2B is good for sketching. Try using pencils of different hardnesses to find those you're most comfortable with. You'll need a sharpener and an eraser of course! You could also use a mechanical pencil.

CURVES

Drawing smooth curves for action lines and speech balloons can be tricky. A set of curves or a circle and ellipse template can help. For perfect circles, use a template or drawing compass.

PAPER

You can draw on any kind of paper, especially for early sketches and planning. For final drafts, professional comic artists use a thick, smooth art paper. Comics are drawn larger than they are printed in comic books.

PENS

Pens are a matter of personal choice. You might try out many different kinds before you find the perfect match. Find a pen that gives you a solid, permanent line. As you grow as a comic artist, you'll want to expand your pen collection. Eventually, you'll need pens of different thicknesses and a marker for filling in large areas.

BRUSHES, FOUNTAIN PENS

Inking over your pencils with a fountain pen or a brush dipped in ink will require some practice and a steady hand, but it can produce great results! A brush will give you more control over the thickness of your lines. Brushes are also good for filling in large areas with black ink that won't fade. You might also like working with brush pens.

STRAIGHT EDGES

You'll need a smooth metal or plastic ruler to draw comic panels and lines for comic book lettering. A triangle is also useful for panel drawing.

Many professional comic artists draw and color their art using tablets and computers. However, when you're just starting to learn and practice comic art skills, nothing beats good old pen and paper. You can get your ideas down while mastering basic techniques.

BODY MATTERS

When you can draw a figure with accurate proportions, your characters will look more realistic. Superheroes and villains often have exaggerated muscular physiques — some may even have animal or alien features!

The human body is symmetrical, with the bones and muscles on the left matching those on the right.

Men's bodies are often wide at the shoulders and chests, then narrower at the hips. Women's bodies are often narrow at the waist and wider at the hips, like the number 8.

All human bodies are about eight heads tall. The waist is about three heads down from the top of the body, and the hands reach midway down the thigh.

TOP TIP

You don't have to give all of your comic book characters an athletic build. Use different heights and body shapes so that readers find it easier to tell them apart.

When you draw a person standing up straight, you should be able to draw a straight line from the top of their head down through their waist, to their knees, and through the center of their feet. Their shoulders should push out as far as their bottom, while their chest pushes out as far as their toes.

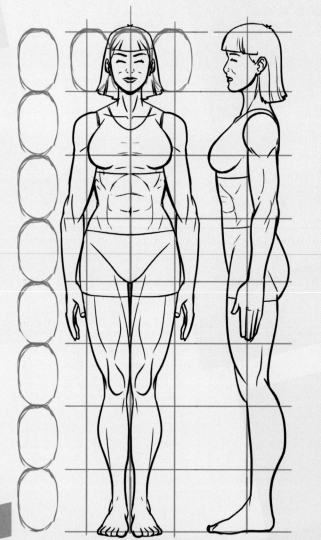

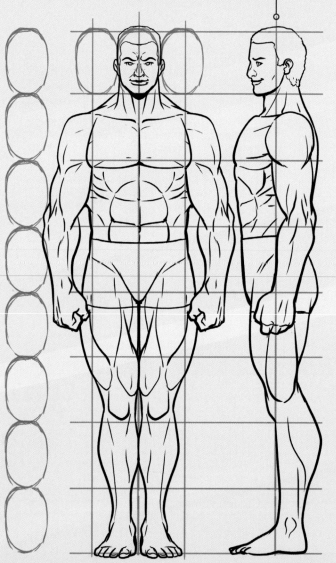

FACE TIME

Faces have their own proportions, with eyes and ears about halfway down the head. Here are average faces you can use for reference.

The ears are about the same height and position as the nose.

The eyes should be one eye-width apart.

Jaws are important to the shape of a person's face. They can be wide and square, narrow and sharp, or round and soft.

The nose forms an imaginary triangle with one point above the nose and one point on either side of the mouth.

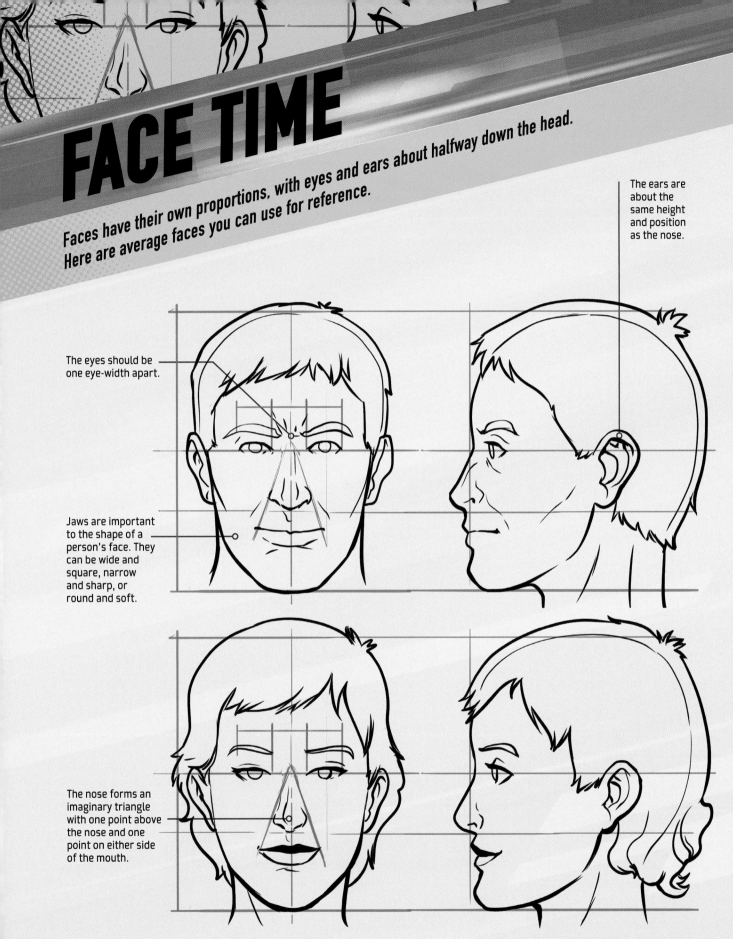

Look at your friends' and family members' faces. You will see many variations. Sketch the details you see and study their hairstyles. You can use traits like these to make each of your comic characters unique.

VILE VILLAINS

Super villains are a lot of fun to create. They can look mean and scary, and carry all kinds of wild-looking weapons. Here are some tips on how to create memorable villains—then let them loose to cause trouble!

BAD BRAINS

You can't go wrong with a mad scientist—they come up with the wildest world-conquering schemes, and their inventions can take your stories in fun and unexpected directions. Let your imagination run wild! While this professor may not look particularly strong, he has all the best gadgets.

NAME: PROFESSOR PAYNE

REAL IDENTITY: Parzival Payne

POWERS: Ultra-intelligent inventor.

ORIGIN: Payne's only friend as a child was his computer. His obsessive studies led him to become a scientific genius with no compassion for people.

STRENGTH ◆◆◇◇◇
INTELLIGENCE ◆◆◆◆◆
SPECIAL POWERS ◆◆◆◆◇
FIGHTING SKILLS ◆◇◇◇◇

SCHEMER

A super-villain team is usually led by the biggest brain, rather than the strongest fighter—someone who can come up with the cleverest ways of defeating heroes and bringing power or wealth to their evil chums. Your villain's greatest power might be how they control other people.

CREEPY COLORS

Killgore has chosen a typically villainous color scheme for his costume — green and purple. Reds, blues, and yellows just seem too bright and positive for a villain.

POSTURE

Note this mutant's menacing pose. Even if you only saw his shadow, you'd know he was creepy! While heroes tend to stand tall and proud, villains like Killgore often skulk, hunch, or pose in a threatening way.

NAME: KILLGORE

REAL IDENTITY: Gordon Kiehl

POWERS: Has claws that can cut through rock and metal.

ORIGIN: Insane rock star Kiehl remixed his own DNA live on stage and grew unbreakable talons. Impossible to imprison, Killgore breaks the law just for the publicity.

STRENGTH ◈◈◈◈◇◇
INTELLIGENCE ◈◈◇◇◇◇
SPECIAL POWERS ◈◈◇◇◇◇
FIGHTING SKILLS ◈◈◈◈◇◇

EVIL OPPOSITE

If you're trying to come up with a villain to take on a hero, imagine what their opposite would be.

Evil cyborg Upgrade could be the mirror image of a hero who uses technology for good — or even of a hero who has beneficial powers over nature.

MOTIVATION

What drives your villain? Upgrade's lack of emotion is what makes her a monster, not her weapons. By cutting off her feelings, she doesn't think about the harm she may cause others. Equally, it is hard to persuade her to stop being a villain.

NAME: UPGRADE

REAL IDENTITY: Paola Barzetti

POWERS: Strong and fast bionic body, blaster weapons.

ORIGIN: Convinced that artificial intelligence would one day rule Earth, Barzetti detached her pain receptors and replaced her human parts with weapon tech.

STRENGTH ◇◇◇◇◇
INTELLIGENCE ◇◇◇◇◇
SPECIAL POWERS ◇◇◇◇◇
FIGHTING SKILLS ◇◇◇◇◇

ACHILLES HEEL

An Achilles heel is a character's weak spot that can be exploited and lead to their downfall. In the case of Brutus, the more he pushes himself to be stronger, the less intelligent he becomes. For heroes to outwit him, they need to find him weak and clever — or they must push the strong version to make a stupid mistake!

NAME: **BRUTUS**

REAL IDENTITY: **Bruce Tuska**

POWERS: The stronger he gets, the dumber he becomes.

ORIGIN: Scientist Tuska, testing a super-strength formula on himself, gained massive power at the expense of his intelligence.

STRENGTH ◆◆◆◆◆
INTELLIGENCE ◆◇◇◇◇
SPECIAL POWERS ◆◆◆◆◇
FIGHTING SKILLS ◆◆◇◇◇

MUSCLE-BOUND

Brutus is super-strong but still needs realistic anatomy. Although you can exaggerate the muscles in a human body, you need to know where they go and what they do. Then it's time to smash!

FEEL THE POWER

The Gauntlet is ready to strike with his symbiotic glove's devastating power bolts. Here's how to draw the bad guy from scratch and fire up his deadly weapon.

NAME: THE GAUNTLET

REAL IDENTITY: Evgeny Blok

POWERS: Wears an alien glove that fires plasma blasts and affects gravity.

ORIGIN: Blok discovered his glove weapon in the wreck of an alien spaceship in Siberia and became possessed by its twisted alien consciousness.

STRENGTH ◆◆◇◇◇
INTELLIGENCE ◆◆◇◇◇
SPECIAL POWERS ◆◆◆◆◇
FIGHTING SKILLS ◆◆◇◇◇

1. WIRE FRAME

Start with a simple figure to show the pose of your villain and the direction in which his head is turned. The Gauntlet is all about his power glove, so his right hand is raised to show it off.

2. BLOCK FIGURE

Fill out the Gauntlet's figure using 3D shapes. Not every character needs to be tall and muscular. Blok is a heavy-set character—he found his weapon by accident and doesn't need to be lean or athletic to use it.

3. ANATOMY

Now work on the villain's anatomy, defining his chest, belly, arm, and leg muscles. You can start to add detail to his alien power glove, too.

4. FINISHED PENCIL SKETCHES

Now the Gauntlet gets his costume. It hangs loose around his padding and boots. Give your villain a mean, unfriendly expression, and add a flare ahead of the glove as it fires.

FEEL THE POWER

HAVING A BLAST!

Power bolts can be drawn in many ways. Here are just a few.

You can have a starburst effect, with rays shooting from an explosive source.

You can have a cosmic power bolt that starts with a splash before becoming thinner and controlled.

Or you can have a mini electrical storm, with a lightning bolt surrounded by electrical charges.

5. INKS

Using ink with a pen or brush, carefully go over the pencil lines you want to keep. The Gauntlet's cap casts a shadow, but his eyes glow bright in the dark to show he is possessed by the glove!

6. COLORS

Time for color! The blast from the glove lights the Gauntlet's costume. The other side of his outfit is in shadow. The contrast of light and dark adds drama to the figure and makes the glove appear even more fearsome.

TOP TIP

When coloring a figure with a strong contrast of light and dark, start with the pale colors, then add the darker tones.

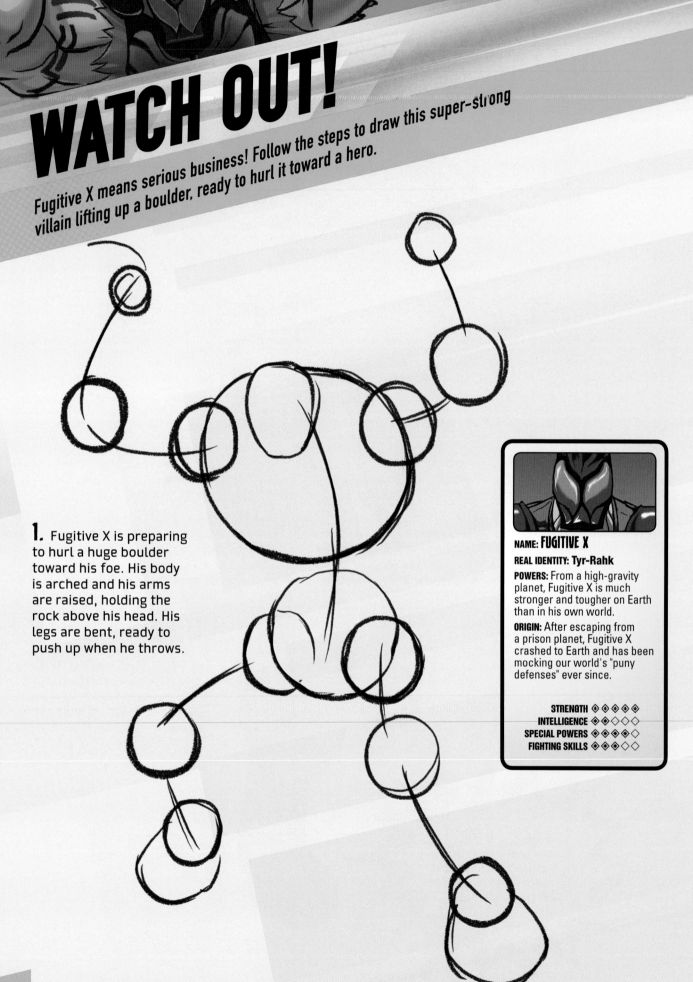

WATCH OUT!

Fugitive X means serious business! Follow the steps to draw this super-strong villain lifting up a boulder, ready to hurl it toward a hero.

1. Fugitive X is preparing to hurl a huge boulder toward his foe. His body is arched and his arms are raised, holding the rock above his head. His legs are bent, ready to push up when he throws.

NAME: FUGITIVE X

REAL IDENTITY: Tyr-Rahk

POWERS: From a high-gravity planet, Fugitive X is much stronger and tougher on Earth than in his own world.

ORIGIN: After escaping from a prison planet, Fugitive X crashed to Earth and has been mocking our world's "puny defenses" ever since.

STRENGTH ◇◇◇◇◇
INTELLIGENCE ◇◇◇◇◇
SPECIAL POWERS ◇◇◇◇◇
FIGHTING SKILLS ◇◇◇◇◇

2. This alien villain has the same anatomy as a human, but he is stronger, with a wide chest and shoulders, and chunky arms and legs.

3. The muscles in Fugitive X's lower arms and thighs are bulging as he supports the weight of the large rock. His padded clothing mimics the muscles underneath. Alien prison tattoos have been added to his arms.

4. In the finished color art, texture has been added to the boulder to make it look rocky. Most of Fugitive X is in shade below it. The dark hues add to his menace.

WEIGHTY WORK

To hold such a heavy weight above his head, Fugitive X needs to balance himself. His **CENTER OF GRAVITY** is shown by a vertical line drawn through a point just behind his belly button to the ground between his feet. For the figure to look balanced, the weight of the rock and his body should be evenly distributed on each side of the line.

SOURCE MATERIAL

Using models and picture references for your drawing isn't cheating. By referring to real life, you'll improve your skills and build up an image bank in your head.

You can learn a lot from studying comics, but it's no substitute for drawing from real life. Ask your friends and family to pose for your drawings.

A mirror is a must! Use yourself as a model to capture tricky facial expressions, hand gestures, and poses.

Keep clippings of useful magazine photos of athletes, fashion, vehicles, and buildings, or search online for reference pictures. Using picture references can improve the **REALISM** in your drawing, but don't let it stop you from using your imagination!

GET THE LOOK

When heroes meet villains, the stakes — and emotions — are high. Practico drawing these facial expressions to show how your characters are really feeling.

FEAR
The brow becomes lined as the eyebrows are raised. The bottom row of teeth is revealed.

ANGER
The eyebrows are lowered, and a wrinkle appears above the nose. Teeth are gritted.

HAPPINESS
The eyebrows and corners of the mouth are raised, creating creases at the sides. The cheeks are pushed up.

SADNESS
The eyes look down. The bottom lip sticks out, and the brow is wrinkled.

SHOCK
The mouth and eyes are wide open, with the eyebrows raised.

DETERMINATION
The eyebrows are lowered in a straight line. Eyes look straight ahead, with the mouth closed tightly.

MANIA
A wide toothy grin, the eyes looking forward, with one raised eyebrow and wrinkles above.

SMASH IT UP!

The Terror Trio — Igniter, Trauma, and Aftershock — are ripping up the streets!
Here's how you can cause destruction, too . . . but only on paper, please!

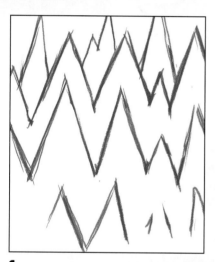

1. To start a fire, lightly pencil **PARALLEL** rows of zigzags, including peaks of different heights.

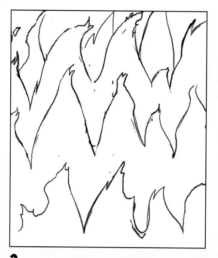

2. Use these lines as guides for drawing curved, **IRREGULAR** flames.

3. Color the flames from white at the base, to yellow, through orange, to red at the top.

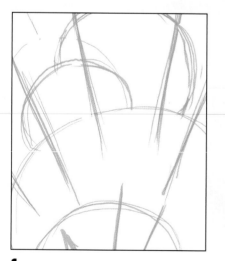

1. For an explosion, lightly pencil curves moving outward from the center of the blast.

2. Connect some of these curves to form a darker cloud around the blast center. Add a few shoots of flame leaping from the fireball.

3. Color the explosion with a dark red outer layer, turning to paler reds and yellows inside, with flashes of white where the blast is hottest.

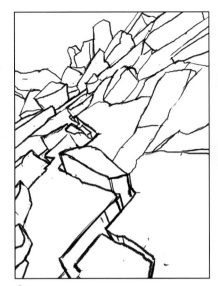

1. For earthquakes, lightly pencil zigzags to show where the ground is breaking. Divide the ground around these lines into irregular shapes, like jigsaw pieces.

2. Now draw a rocky edge on each broken piece of ground to show that it has been raised. Choose different edges and angles for each piece.

3. For the finished destruction, rough and rocky texture has been added to the broken pieces of ground, with more cracks and a few stones jumping into the air.

NAME: TRAUMA

REAL IDENTITY: Spike Tucker

POWERS: Hurls balls of energy that cause explosions where they hit.

ORIGIN: Surviving a quantum bomb blast, Tucker absorbed its energy and became able to transmit it as small explosions.

STRENGTH ◆◆◆◆◇◇
INTELLIGENCE ◆◆◆◇◇◇
SPECIAL POWERS ◆◆◆◆◇◇
FIGHTING SKILLS ◆◆◆◆◇◇

NAME: IGNITER

REAL IDENTITY: Roisin Byrne

POWERS: Able to turn a spark into raging flames.

ORIGIN: As a youth, Byrne got into trouble for causing fires. Later, she discovered she was a mutant with power over plasma.

STRENGTH ◆◆◆◆◇◇
INTELLIGENCE ◆◆◆◆◇◇
SPECIAL POWERS ◆◆◆◆◇◇
FIGHTING SKILLS ◆◆◆◆◆◇

ORIGIN: The temperamental and disgraced scientist Lennox developed a costume that converts his rage into an earthquake-creating force.

NAME: AFTERSHOCK

REAL IDENTITY: Dr. Zane Lennox

POWERS: Causes violent tremors through touch when angry.

STRENGTH ◆◆◆◆◇◇
INTELLIGENCE ◆◆◇◇◇◇
SPECIAL POWERS ◆◆◆◆◇◇
FIGHTING SKILLS ◆◆◆◆◇◇

DEADLY DEVICES

Super villains are always coming up with new dangerous weapons, from blastors to heavy-duty tanks. Get to grips with the art of menacing machinery.

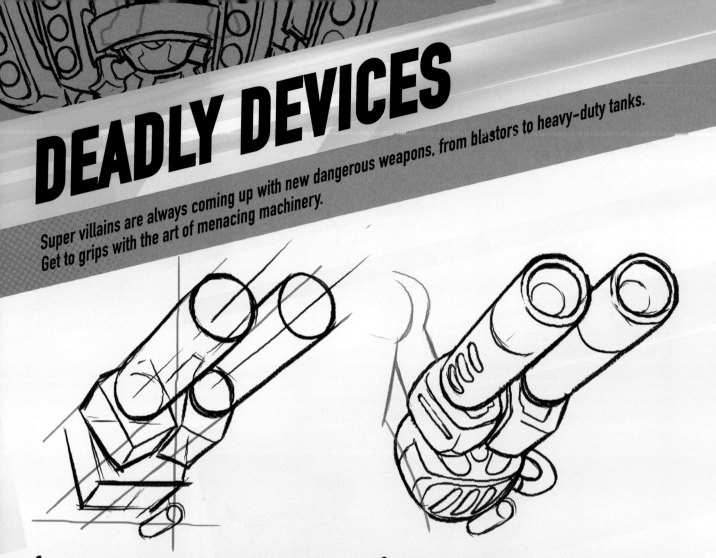

1. Upgrade's double-barreled atomic disruptor is based around two **CYLINDERS**. Lightly sketch these, using **PERSPECTIVE** lines as a guide, then add other 3D shapes to build up the device.

2. In the finished pencil sketch, the corners of the 3D shapes are smooth and a power cable, lights, and vents have been added.

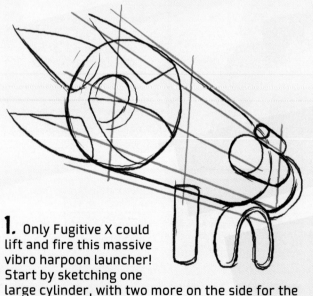

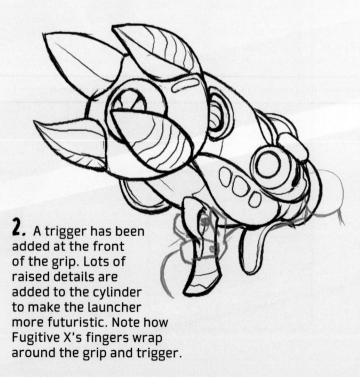

1. Only Fugitive X could lift and fire this massive vibro harpoon launcher! Start by sketching one large cylinder, with two more on the side for the sights. Add points to the front of the barrel, plus a handgrip and shoulder rest below it.

2. A trigger has been added at the front of the grip. Lots of raised details are added to the cylinder to make the launcher more futuristic. Note how Fugitive X's fingers wrap around the grip and trigger.

26

1. Professor Payne has his own personal attack platform, armed to the teeth with blasters and rocket launchers. First sketch the base for Payne to stand on, with a raised front and steering column. Add rectangular fins and blocks for the weapons on each side.

2. In the pencil sketches, the 3D shapes and platform front are more curved. Each blaster array is aimed forward, with a heat vent at the rear. Consider how the mad professor will fit on his attack platform.

Now turn the page to see how these weapons are used in the final scene!

TOTAL DESTRUCTION

With mighty weapons in the hands of criminals, Capital City is at the mercy of those monstrous megalomaniacs! Someone call the superheroes!

THE REIGN OF HUMANS WILL SOON BE OVER!

HANDS UP!

A successful villain may rub his hands in glee, point, punch, or brandish a weapon. Hands can seem hard to draw at first — here are some simple steps for getting them just right.

OPEN HAND

Start by drawing a round-edged square for the palm. RADIATING from this, add lines following each finger and thumb bone. Check the finger lengths against your own hand. Draw circles for the joints, then an outline around these to form the shape of the fingers and thumb. Add lines on the palm and one or two wrinkles on each finger and thumb joint.

CLAW

Start by drawing the palm as a flat box, with four curved lines for the fingers and one hooked thumb. Add circles for the finger and thumb joints. Now draw the outlines for all the fingers and thumbs around these, adding sharp fingernails at the end.

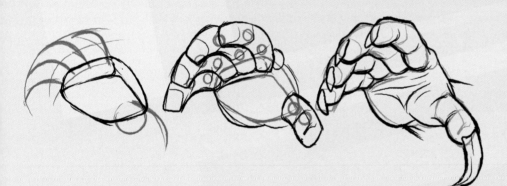

GRIPPING BACK OF HAND

Start by drawing the back of the hand as a small, flat box. Add lines showing the position of the gripping fingers, plus circles for the knuckles. Now draw the outlines for all the fingers, with wrinkles on the joints.

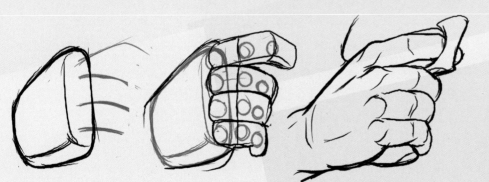

GLOSSARY

CENTER OF GRAVITY The point from which the weight of a body is said to act. On a figure, this is behind the belly button.

CYLINDER A solid shape with parallel sides and a circular cross-section.

IRREGULAR Uneven, not following an even pattern or arrangement.

PARALLEL Two lines running in the same direction, at an equal distance apart.

PERSPECTIVE A way of representing three-dimensional (3D) objects in a picture.

POSTURE The way that you stand or sit.

RADIATING Spreading out from.

REALISM How much a picture or other representation looks like the real thing.

FURTHER INFORMATION

Books to read

Create Your Own Superhero Stories by Paul Moran (Buster Books, 2010)

DC Comics Coloring Book by DC Comics Warner Bros. (Studio Press, 2016)

Drawing Manga: Step by Step by Ben Krefta (Arcturus Publishing, 2013)

Stan Lee's How to Draw Superheroes by Stan Lee (Watson-Guptill, 2013)

The Super Book for Super-Heroes by Jason Ford (Laurence King, 2013)

Write and Draw Your Own Comics by Louise Stowell and Jess Bradley (Usborne, 2014)

Websites

PowerKids Press has developed an online list of websites related to the subject of this book. This site is updated regularly. Please use this link to access the list: **www.powerkidslinks.com/uca/villains**

INDEX

Published in 2018 by **The Rosen Publishing Group, Inc.**
29 East 21st Street, New York, NY 10010

CATALOGING-IN-PUBLICATION DATA

Names: Potter, William.
Title: Drawing dangerous villains / William Potter and Juan Calle.
Description: New York : PowerKids Press, 2018. | Series: Ultimate comic art | Includes index.
Identifiers: ISBN 9781508154723 (pbk.) | ISBN 9781508154662 (library bound) | ISBN 9781508154549 (6 pack)
Subjects: LCSH: Villains in art--Juvenile literature. | Figure drawing--Technique--Juvenile literature. |
    Comic books, strips, etc.--Technique--Juvenile literature.
Classification: LCC NC825.V54 P68 2018 | DDC 741.5'1--dc23

Text: William Potter
Illustrations: Juan Calle and Info Liberum
Design: Neal Cobourne
Design series edition: Emma Randall
Editor: Joe Harris

Manufactured in the United States of America

CPSIA Compliance Information: Batch BS17PK: For Further Information contact Rosen Publishing, New York, New York at 1-800-237-9932.